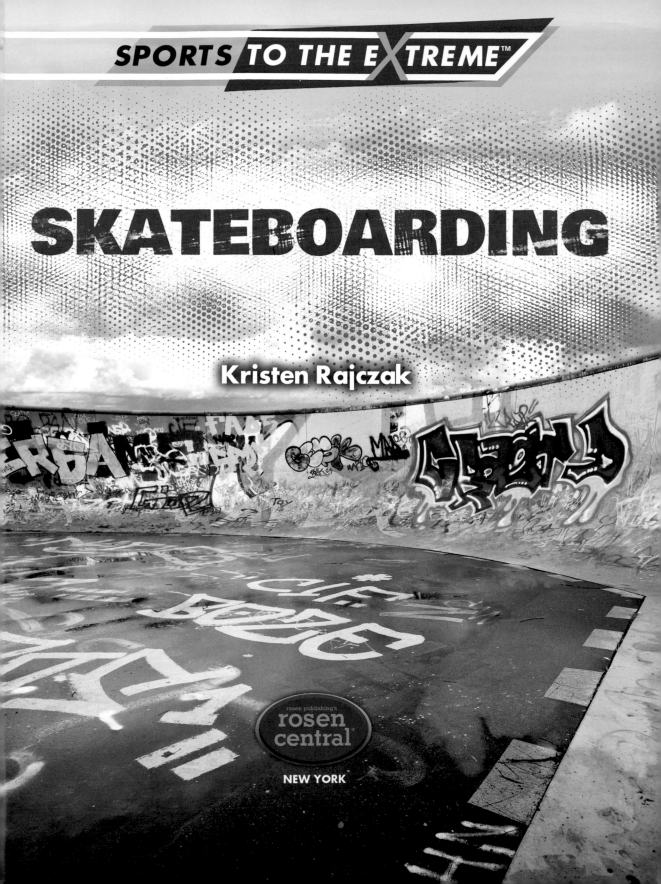

SPORTS **TO THE EXTREME**™

SKATEBOARDING

Kristen Rajczak

rosen publishing's
**rosen
central**

NEW YORK

Published in 2016 by The Rosen Publishing Group, Inc.
29 East 21st Street, New York, NY 10010

Copyright © 2016 by The Rosen Publishing Group, Inc.

First Edition

Library of Congress Cataloging-in-Publication Data

Rajczak, Kristen.
Skateboarding/Kristen Rajczak.—First Edition.
pages cm.—(Sports to the Extreme)
Includes bibliographical references and index.
ISBN 978-1-4994-3569-6 (Library bound)—ISBN 978-1-4994-3571-9 (Paperback)—
ISBN 978-1-4994-3572-6 (6-pack)
1. Skateboarding—Juvenile literature. I. Title.
GV859.8.R35 2016
796.22—dc23

2014044183

Manufactured in the United States of America

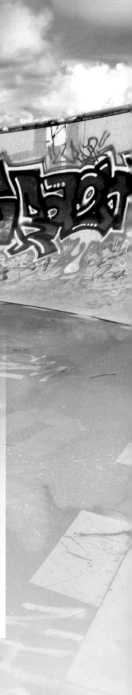

CONTENTS

Introduction   4

CHAPTER ONE
A History of Ups and Downs   **6**

CHAPTER TWO
Boards and Bruises   **13**

CHAPTER THREE
Innovation: The Ollie and Beyond   **23**

CHAPTER FOUR
Free Skate   **31**

Glossary   40
For More Information   41
For Further Reading   44
Bibliography   45
Index   46

INTRODUCTION

Tony Hawk had already failed seven times when he stood on top of the vert at the fifth annual X Games in 1999. He was trying to land a "900"—a two-and-a-half rotation spin—in the Vert Best Trick contest. He'd fallen off his board time and again; each attempt could have led to a career-ending injury. But on the eighth attempt—his last—Hawk skated up each side of the ramp once before spinning into action and landing on his board with a deep knee bend at the end of the trick. Jono Schwan, another pro skateboarder, described the feat to ESPN.com in 2014: "The reason Tony's 900 was so incredible was that most thought it was impossible to do, like getting a man to the moon."

Perhaps the most influential trick in modern skateboarding, Hawk's 900 inspired a generation of skateboarders. Pro skateboarder Tom Schaar was born the year Hawk landed the 900. In 2011, Schaar became the youngest skater ever to land the trick. He saw Hawk's trick on a video and told ESPN.com, "It inspired me to skate vert instead of street. It kind of launched my whole skating career." In 2012, at age twelve, Schaar became the first skateboarder to land a 1080.

Tony Hawk is one of the best-known skaters in the world for a reason. He's mastered innovative tricks!

There's no keeping up with the progress of skateboarding tricks today because they can happen anywhere. While pros are competing for big purses, a kid with a hand-me-down skateboard can be trying a daring new trick at a local skate park. That's one of the most extreme parts of skateboarding—it's possible for anyone to try. And that means anyone can try for the impossible, too. It's this outlook that led Hawk to the top of the sport in 1999 and what will take others there in years to come.

CHAPTER ONE

A HISTORY OF UPS AND DOWNS

The very first skateboards hit the streets in the early twentieth century. They were homemade, usually just boards with roller-skate wheels attached to the bottom and a crate attached to the top for handles. It looked somewhat like a crude scooter. However, skateboards as they're known today came about in California during the 1950s. Many surfers began "surfing the streets" on homemade boards around roughly the same time. In fact, it's not known who first came up with the idea! Again, wooden boards with roller-skate wheels were common.

The first skateboard was sold commercially in 1959. By 1963, the sport was so popular that skateboarders started competing in the first skateboarding competitions.

Since the 1960s, skateboards have been available for anyone to buy.

Nothing like the trick-heavy competitions of today, these early competitions included downhill races and a freestyle event. However, just two years later, the sport's popularity came to a screeching halt. Some of this had to do with the incredible number of injuries among amateur skateboarders. Safety concerns were raised about the clay wheels then manufactured for commercial skateboards. The wheels would break if they hit the ground too hard and were generally hard to control. The growing skateboarding companies closed, and the whole phenomenon was written off as simply a fad.

None of the extreme tricks daring skateboarders attempt today would have become possible without the invention of urethane skateboard wheels. In 1972, Cadillac Wheels came out with the first of these, reigniting interest in skateboarding. The new wheels were the start of the upswing in the popularity of skateboarding in the 1970s. The first skate park was built in 1976 in Florida, followed by a slew of others all around the world. As more were built, skateboarders suddenly had a dedicated space to practice their craft—but these early skate parks played a very small role in the growth of the action sport skateboarding has become. In fact, the high insurance costs of these parks led mainstream skateboarding into another slump.

With the first skate parks came the first places specially reserved for skaters to perfect their craft.

THE Z-BOYS

In 1975, a skateboarding contest was held in Del Mar, California. A team of twelve surfers, called the Zephyr team after a local surf shop, competed—and won—in a sport they did mostly as a hobby. They rode their boards with their knees bent deeply and dragged their hands over the pavement below, as if they were riding a surfboard. The new style of the "Z-Boys," who came from a poor part of California called Dogtown, created a new buzz in skateboarding.

While the Z-Boys competed in the downhill event, where their low-riding techniques seemed really beneficial for going fast, it was their freestyle performances that really made an impact. During the 1970s, freestyle skateboarding was a bit like ice-skating, but on a skateboard. The Z-Boys, unlike other skateboarders, hadn't seriously trained for the competition. A huge drought in that part of California left a lot of swimming pools empty. They would sneak into public pools and backyards and skate there. The unique shape of the pools brought about the new way of riding that the Z-Boys showed off in Del Mar and later. Their style was a clear precursor to today's trick-full vert contests.

The Zephyr team stayed together to compete for only a few months after the Del Mar event in 1975. Several continued professional skateboarding and shaped the modern sport, including Stacy Peralta, Jay Adams, and Tony Alva.

Another construct, one specifically *not* made for skateboarding, inspired creativity in a way skate parks of the 1970s didn't: the empty swimming pool.

IT STARTED WITH THE OLLIE

Following the Z-Boys' legendary performances born out of swimming pool skate sessions, pro skateboarding became a much more serious endeavor. Excitement about what the sport would become grew. It was time to explore the vertical, or "vert," possibilities of skateboarding. Swimming pools gave way to the first ramps, and the first modern skateboarding trick—the ollie—was invented in 1978. Without the ollie, the most exciting tricks of today would not have happened. And without mastering the ollie, skateboarders cannot hope to move on to other such moves.

Nonetheless, one small trick couldn't maintain the sport's mainstream popularity. Concerns about safety again seemed to take skateboarding off the map, though it actually just became

To daring skateboarders of the 1970s, the vert possibilities seemed endless!

more underground. During the 1980s, another kind of skating emerged, likely because skate parks and designated locations for skaters weren't as readily available. Just like the vert skating in swimming pools, street style skateboarding grew out of necessity. Boarders used the existing streetscape to try out new tricks. From curbs and railings to hilly streets, the whole world became a skate park. The graceful freestyle of the skate events of the past gave way to an aggressive and daring skating that any kid with a board could do anywhere.

VIDEO STARS

During the late 1980s, skateboarding's underground following began to grow. Boarders began making videos of their sessions and tricks, and these videos started circulating and inspiring kids and teens to pick up the sport again. One of these video stars became perhaps the biggest pro skateboarding star of all time: Tony Hawk. Hawk teamed up with the Z-Boys' Stacy Peralta, Rodney Mullen, and others to create the Bones Brigade Video Show. The most famous of these videos came out in 1987, titled *The Search for Animal Chin.* The

Bones Brigade's notoriety helped pros such as Hawk become well known. Nonetheless, the late 1980s and early 1990s were a tough time for pro skateboarders trying to make money. It wasn't until the mid-1990s that skateboarding finally broke out beyond the confines of its cult following and reached the national consciousness of America.

Z-Boys star Jay Adams started skating and surfing at a very young age. The Z-Boys' videos helped popularize street skating in the 1980s.

EXTREME GAMES

While the general public had largely forgotten about skateboarding during the late 1980s and early 1990s, boarders had become much better at pulling off tricks. The tricks looked cleaner and were done more efficiently as pros and amateurs alike worked hard on their skills. In addition, vert skating, begun by the Z-Boys in empty California pools, moved into specially constructed half-pipes about 12 feet (3.6 meters) high. Skateboarders started trying their best street style tricks at the top of the half-pipe, showcasing it as a place to get creative.

Then, TV sports network ESPN realized that it was missing out on the ratings that could arise from a whole group of viewers who didn't watch the typical baseball and basketball games. These viewers weren't interested in *SportsCenter* highlighting the best football plays of the weekend. Instead, this demographic—known to be primarily males in their teenage years or twenties—was looking for the thrill of catching air on a skateboard, a snowboard, or a BMX bike. They were seen as a group of not only untapped viewers but also untapped consumers. As a result, ESPN created the Extreme Games, which debuted in 1995, a competition pitting the best "action sports" stars against one another.

The Extreme Games were an extreme success, so much so that the network changed its original plan of having the games every two years to making them an annual event. The name was also changed to the X Games, as that was thought to be friendlier to international audiences. Over time, the X Games became *the* place to show off the coolest, most dangerous tricks that skateboarders could perform. As the X Games were quite prominently televised, kids began growing up in awe of big air, multiple rotations, flips, and handstands—a far cry from the simple downhill slalom events of the 1960s and 1970s. The young, daring personalities progressing skateboarding today often cut their teeth on classic 1990s X Games footage, such as Tony Hawk's famed 900. The X Games brought skateboarding and other extreme sports from the underground into America's living rooms.

CHAPTER TWO

BOARDS AND BRUISES

A new skateboarder might start out with just a board. While that's the most important piece of gear needed to skateboard, the need for others becomes increasingly clear after a few falls. And there will be more than a few!

EVOLUTION OF THE SKATEBOARD

The trick skateboards most people use are about 32 inches (81 centimeters) long and 9 inches (23 cm) wide. Skateboards have three parts. The deck is the board that the skater stands on. The trucks are the T-shaped axles to which the wheels are attached. The wheels are the third part. The introduction of urethane wheels in 1972 was the first change to skateboards that made them safer and better to ride for everyone, from amateurs to pros. Other changes in skateboards have contributed to the popularity of skateboarding, making the ride safer and smoother or creating opportunities for the invention of new tricks.

The earliest commercial skateboards had a flat deck made of wood. By the 1970s, they would be made of aluminum,

13

A key feature of a skateboard deck is the kicktail—the slightly turned-up end that helps skaters perform tricks.

fiberglass, and even plastic. In 1969, decks began being manufactured with a kicktail, or one end of the board slightly turned up. This change made the invention of the ollie possible, and thus, many other tricks. The kicktail also gave skaters a way to stop and control their boards better. Today, many skateboards have a double kicktail, allowing skaters to do more tricks from each side of the board. The rest of the deck isn't totally flat anymore either. During the 1980s, a slight dip in the middle of the deck evolved to help boarders stay on better.

Colorfully designed decks are one way for skateboarders to show their creativity and personality. Like the surfboards after which they were modeled, skateboards often have pictures and words on their underside. Many boarders become known for using a specific brand of skateboard, whose logo is showed off every time they do a trick.

The trucks of the skateboard are very important. They allow skateboarders to turn well—but they didn't start out that way. The first trucks were the same ones used for roller skates. While they did attach the wheels to the deck, boarders couldn't turn at all. The only option was to move in a straight line! In 1973, Bennett Trucks released trucks made specifically for skateboards. Then, in 1978, Indepen-

Without changes in skateboards' trucks, many tricks and turns wouldn't be possible.

dent Trucks improved that design to give boarders an even better turning radius and smoother ride. The mid-1970s also brought about precision ball bearings for skateboard wheels, which made the ride smoother than the loose ball bearings previously used.

Vert and street skateboards aren't the only kinds of boards that benefitted from these changes. Some skateboarders ride their boards off-road—sometimes called mountainboarding or dirtboarding— and need bigger tires and a larger board. Skateboarders are often strapped to the board, too. Downhill skateboarders interested in speed or just simply traveling from place to place often use a longboard. As their name implies, longboards are longer than trick skateboards. They also have larger wheels. Beginning skateboarders often start on a longboard so they have a little extra room to move around and a bit more balance.

Skateboards continue to improve today. They've become more streamlined since the 1970s and are lighter and stronger.

SAFETY FIRST

Skateboarders, even the pros, need other gear besides a board to skate successfully. That's because skateboarders fall a lot! In fact, most people should learn *how* to fall before they even set foot on a board for the first time.

Perhaps the most important piece of gear skateboarders wear is a helmet. The helmet is so important that there's one made specifically for skateboarding that you should buy. Elbow pads and knee pads as well as wrist guards protect skateboarders from the hard falls onto hands and knees that accompany trying a new trick or hitting some rough terrain. Many skateboarders also wear mouth guards to protect their teeth.

Some skateboarding gear might not be the most fashionable to wear outside of the skate park or vert ramp, but skateboarding shoes have become a big part of skate culture and beyond. The bottoms

SKATEBOARDING SAFETY TIPS

Wearing the right gear and having a good quality skateboard are good first steps to being safe while skateboarding. Here are a few other tips to keep in mind before you hop on:

- Skateboarders can be killed if they collide with cars. Be careful when sharing the road, and look into driveways when riding on the sidewalk.
- Only one rider should be atop a skateboard at any time.
- Always check your board before you ride. If anything looks damaged, get it fixed before you ride again.
- Make sure all your gear fits properly, especially your helmet.
- Be aware of the surface on which you're riding. Stones in the road or dips in the sidewalk can send you flying.
- Avoid skateboarding in the rain or at night. You are less visible to other people and can't see where you're going as well.
- Stay in shape in other ways. Keeping your body physically fit will help you complete bigger and better tricks. It will also help prevent injuries.
- Don't wear headphones while skating. You need to be able to hear oncoming cars and other sounds around you.

of a pair of skateboarding shoes should have a good grip so you don't slip. During the 1970s, the shoe company Vans put out a pair of sneakers with vulcanized rubber soles that turned out to be perfect for skateboarding. They weren't made for skateboarding specifically then, but today they sure are! Not only do many pro skateboarders wear Vans, but Vans has become a huge sponsor of extreme sports events, and the shoes have an iconic look for those who like skate style.

EXTREME INJURIES

Though modern skateboards and gear have certainly made skateboarding a safer sport than it was in the 1960s and 1970s, all kinds of skateboarding may result in injury.

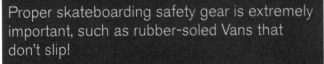

Proper skateboarding safety gear is extremely important, such as rubber-soled Vans that don't slip!

Some injuries are inevitable. One-third of skateboarding injuries happen to those who have been skateboarding for less than a week. Nonetheless, bruises and scrapes are common among experienced skateboarders who are trying new tricks or taking daring—and potentially dangerous—leaps over curbs, cars, or railings, too. Wrist sprains or fractures are the most common types of skateboarding injury. Head injuries, including concussions, and broken teeth and noses are also common. If you're not wearing a helmet and you fall and hit your head, brain injuries could occur.

It's smart to know your limitations as a skateboarder because of how easily you can be injured. Don't try tricks or terrain that are too difficult for your skill level. That's not to say you shouldn't attempt tricks! Just make sure you wear the right safety gear, have a more experienced boarder help you, and learn the basics before transitioning into harder moves.

Harder tricks mean harder falls, even for the best skateboarders. When Australian boarder Jake Brown lost his board during his session on the Mega Ramp at the 2007 X Games, he told MTV News that he "had plenty of time to think about what was going to happen" while he fell from about 45 feet (13.7 m). An experienced skateboarder, Brown knew he had to turn his body so that more than one part of him would hit the ground. He'd seen another boarder, Pat Duffy, fall from that height before, and Duffy shattered a bone in one of his legs because that's the only body part on which he landed. Brown lost consciousness for eight full minutes after the fall. He was lucky to leave the games with his life, though he also left with a concussion, one sprained wrist, one broken wrist, a bruised liver, and whiplash, among other injuries.

Pro skateboarder Bob Burnquist took a bad fall at the 2012 X Games. He still won first place!

After his death-defying crash, Brown became one of the most recognizable skateboarders in the world. Not only did he survive the fall, he walked off the ramp to cheers and applause. Injuries like his can become somewhat celebrated by the skateboarding culture, which may give young boarders the wrong message. Taking risks when you're prepared for them can result in some of the most extreme tricks and most fun skating sessions. However, injuries such as Brown's shouldn't be aspired to. Injuries will occur in skateboarding—but they don't make you any more "extreme" if they happen because you aren't using common sense. They could quickly end your time on the board.

CHAPTER THREE

INNOVATION: THE OLLIE AND BEYOND

Alan Gelfand—nicknamed "Ollie"—invented the very first skateboarding trick in 1978. He slammed his back foot onto the kicktail of his board while jumping up, popping both himself and his board into the air. The trick was called an "ollie" after Gelfand and became the basis for the many complex tricks that came after it. The ollie is commonly the first trick new boarders learn, and it's the trick to master before moving on to something harder. The invention of the ollie was a big part of the transitions from the freestyle and slalom skateboarding styles of the 1960s and 1970s to the vert and street events that are still around today.

From a simple ollie, skaters learned to do 180s, or half turns. After 180s became old hat, skateboarders tried 360s—and kept going! The kickflip was followed by the heelflip, in which a skater pushes the front of the board down so that it spins until he or she lands. These are just two examples of how skateboarders build on the tricks they know to improve and create new moves.

23

Learning new tricks, such as this kick flip, often takes a lot of practice.

MARK GONZALES

In 2013, Mark Gonzales was named the number one most influential skateboarder by *Transworld Skateboarding* magazine, one of the most popular skateboarding magazines. Though he's not as well known to the general public as other skate legends, "Gonz" was heralded by *Huck* magazine as "practically the inventor" of street style skating.

Gonzales grew up near Los Angeles, California, amid the popularity of the Z-Boys and their pool-riding ways. By the time he was a teenager, skate parks with big ramps and pipes had popped up—but so did a lot of injuries (and then insurance prices). As these parks started closing up during the early 1980s, skateboarders were looking for new ways to keep riding. Gonz, from the start, was at the forefront of the new way to skate. In a February 2013 article, pro skateboarder Lance Mountain told *Huck* magazine about watching Gonz ride from the bus stop to his house: "He rode away from the car, up the curb, down the street, the way we would ride a pool... And people didn't do that on the street back them." Mountain said Gonz seemed to use the "flow" of vert riding—which emulated surfing—on the street. "[Gonz] is arguably the most important skateboarder to live because he redefined what it became," Mountain said.

Gonz was known for skating on whatever he encountered on the street. As the 1980s came to an end, his style of skating was gathering momentum. Gonz started the skate company Blind Skateboards in 1989 and released videos of himself and others doing tricks no one had previously seen. *Video Days*, released in 1991, was a particularly note-worthy video.

In a July 2012 article, James Guida of the *New Yorker* summarized Gonzales: "Where people saw un-rideable things—a long, zigzagging handrail, for instance, or two thin benches separated by a foot-long gap—Gonz saw ingenious new possibilities and realized them without a further thought." Gonz was talented, but it was his sense of imagination that made him an incredible skateboarder and a great influence on the sport as it is today.

GO BIG, OR GO HOME

Tony Hawk's 900 in the 1999 X Games was incredibly influential to the skateboarding community because it proved that something thought to be impossible truly wasn't with hard work and daring. Since then, many other skateboarders have attempted thrilling tricks in skate parks, the X Games best trick contest, and even one of the world's natural wonders.

BOB BURNQUIST

Extreme tricks can't be discussed without bringing up Bob Burnquist. At one point, he had the biggest Mega Ramp (a huge vert ramp) on earth in his backyard!

Burnquist created the Loop of Death in 2002. It looked like a roller coaster loop in which the skater would enter at one end and sail around the loop upside down on the board. But the incredible speed, balance, and fearlessness of completing that loop weren't enough for

Bob Burnquist turned pro at age fourteen. He's competed in the biggest skateboarding events all over the world since.

Burnquist. He made a top portion of the loop on a hinge so it could be opened. Any skater who attempts it has to clear a gap upside down! After several tries, Burnquist landed the Loop of Death with a gap to win the title of King of Skate. Tony Hawk, however, once fractured his skull attempting this trick.

Then, in 2006, Burnquist decided to jump 1,600 feet (487.6 m) into the Grand Canyon. A combination skateboarding trick and BASE jump, the stunt began with Burnquist speeding down a 40-foot-tall (12-m) ramp and grinding down a 40-foot steel rail. He was, of course, the first to complete this extreme trick. He told *Outside* magazine, "This definitely ranks among the coolest things I've ever done."

CATCHING SOME AIR

In 2011, a trick by Aaron "Jaws" Homoki made headlines in the skateboarding world. According to *Thrasher* magazine, "by height, distance, or any other measure" Homoki's jump over a flight of twenty concrete stairs was the "biggest ollie ever."

Another flight of stairs has become famous because of the skateboarders attempting new, extreme ways to descend it. The twenty concrete stairs at El Toro High School in Lake Forest, California, are steep and divided

Aaron "Jaws" Homoki had to have a lot of daring to attempt his huge ollie. As daring and extreme as skateboarding tricks can be, skateboarders should always be mindful of safety and wear the appropriate gear—especially a helmet—every time they step foot on a board.

by a railing that invites long rail slides. It's been featured in many ways, many times in skate videos. In 2006, a particularly daring skateboarder named Dave didn't just jump the stairs—he attempted a kickflip, too. That means that Bachinsky had a lot more to worry about when it came to landing. When doing a kickflip, a skateboarder first does an ollie, but then uses his foot to spin the board underneath him and then stop the spin, ultimately landing with his feet on the board. Bachinsky had to do this while hurtling down the famed drop of the El Toro stairs. He did it, but it took twelve tries. Luckily, he wasn't hurt too badly on the first eleven attempts.

SKATE CULTURE AND STYLE

What's behind skaters' need to do bigger and better tricks? Why encourage more death-defying rotations and incredible speed? Skateboarding culture, from its beginning, has played a big role in the sport itself. Many of the stereotypes associated with surfers carried over to skateboarders. Often, they were seen as criminals, thought to disregard people's property. Pool riding—or trespassing as some called it—contributed to this image, as did the marks skaters left from grinding or jumping off the streetscape of cities. Because of this, skateboarding outside of certain areas was illegal in many cities. A popular bumper sticker from the 1980s read, "Skateboarding Is Not a Crime" (even though it was in some places!). Laws banning skateboarding often grew out of safety concerns as well. To those drawn to the daring stunts of skateboarding, nothing could have made the sport more appealing than being told to stop or be more careful.

The rebellion around skate culture grew in tandem with the U.S. punk rock music scene of the late 1980s and early 1990s. The music's antiestablishment bent fueled frustrated skaters while the musicians influenced how skaters began to dress. Today, the popular skateboarding "look" is easy to spot—long shorts, colorful graphic t-shirts, flat-brimmed hats with graffiti-style lettering. Brands such as Vans, Hurley, and DC are ever-present at the X Games, both as sponsors and as fashion.

Today, the skater look is common *outside* of the skate park, too! What was once an expression of rebellion can now be found at every mall in the United States. Luckily, experimenting with new tricks and news ways of riding the board keeps the freedom of the early days of skateboarding alive and well.

PRAISE FOR INNOVATION

In a 2013 press release, Jeffrey Brodie, deputy director of the Smithsonian Institute's Lemelson Center for the Study of Invention and Innovation, said: "Skateboarding is surrounded by a culture of inventive creativity and imaginations. Skateboarders are similar to inventors in viewing the world from a unique perspective—what it has potential to be." Brodie was speaking about the sport because, at the time, the Smithsonian was putting on an event celebrating donations from famous boarders to its collection of skateboarding artifacts.

Tony Hawk donated his first skateboard, which had belonged to his brother. Rodney Mullen and Cindy Whitehead—a professional female skater active in the 1970s—also made donations. Mullen and Hawk spoke at the event about trick innovation, while Whitehead spoke about skater fashion and how it has bled into popular styles. According to ESPN, Hawk said the event seemed to mark a "new era" in skateboarding: "I can't believe skateboarding has come this far, or that an esteemed museum would even be interested in my skateboard."

Skateboarding is still illegal on many streets, though, due to past destruction caused by boarders and the dangers of sharing streets with cars. Where can the innovation spoken about at the Smithsonian continue? In 2009, Portland, Oregon, seemed to be leading the charge with designated "skate routes" marked throughout the city and a plan to build nineteen skate parks within its bounds before 2020. While this seems positive, the *Wall Street Journal* pointed out that, "Portland's skate park system is just the biggest example of how skateboarders are institutionalizing their sport." It's clear that the inherent creative nature of skateboarding culture can't thrive as it once did without some institutional help.

CHAPTER FOUR

FREE SKATE

For most of the existence of the sport, no dominant governing body has been established to oversee skateboarding as a whole, something that makes sense given the antiestablishment culture from which the sport originally grew. Nevertheless, that doesn't mean that people aren't trying.

ORGANIZED FREEDOM

World Cup Skateboarding, Street League Skateboarding, and the International Skateboarding Federation are all groups that aim, in some way or another, to be the ultimate governing body for pro skateboarding worldwide. World Cup oversees the largest competitions around the world, complete with a skater ranking system and a detailed rulebook. Street League Skateboarding, founded in 2010 by pro skateboarder Rob Dyrdek, is responsible for a tour run in conjunction with Nike SB (Nike's line of skateboarding shoes). On its website, Street League Skateboarding states that its mission is "to foster growth, popularity and acceptance of street skateboarding worldwide." The

Huge crowds head to skateboarding competitions around the world. Who knows where the next big trick will happen!

International Skateboarding Federation and World Governing Body (ISF) seeks to have a slightly different role; it is less focused on the competition aspect and focuses more on maintaining the integrity of the sport and its promotion worldwide.

None of these organizations has yet reached the level of other sports' governing bodies, such as the NFL for football or FIFA for soccer. There remains a risky, exciting element to skateboarding—which some feel a governing body would limit. The ISF even acknowledges this, stating in its mission that it wants "to guarantee skateboarding continues to provide the freedom of self-expression and creativity"—a goal that, in other sports, could run counter to rules about how tricks are done or when new tricks can be introduced to competition.

THE OLYMPICS

One reason some deem a world governing body necessary for skateboarding is the Olympics. Without one authoritative group advocating for the sport that is accepted by the International Olympic Committee, skateboarding is unlikely ever to be included in the Olympic Games. In addition, if it is not a group respected by the majority of skateboarders and with a grasp on both the sport and its culture, then skateboarding is unlikely to be included in the Olympics in a way that many pro skateboarders would agree with.

In 2004, the ISF formed partially for this purpose. In the United States, USA Skateboarding formed in 2003 to be the national

RESENTING THE ESTABLISHMENT

Creating the ISF and USA Skateboarding to represent skateboarders in the Olympic talks assumes that pro skateboarders even *want* to be included in the Olympic Games. ESPN once quoted Tony Hawk as having said, "The Olympics need us more than we need them." The Olympics often try to stay relevant, and a demographically young sport such as skateboarding could bring in more interest and viewership among young people. The success of slopestyle and freeskiing in the 2014 Winter Olympics again opened the conversation about the similar sport of skateboarding.

Could skateboarding even fit into the Olympic mold? Gary Ream, the president of USA Skateboarding, wanted it to be called an "exhibition" instead of a sport. Dave Carnie, executive director of USA Skateboarding, told ESPN that skateboarders wearing uniforms and taking drug tests would be "delightfully ridiculous."

The competition aspect seems especially troublesome. Neal Hendrix of the ISF worried that people outside the world of skateboarding might make decisions on how skaters would be judged, what kinds of courses they'd compete on, and how qualification would be measured. Skateboarding is sometimes considered an art, and judging it as one would gymnastics or figure skating (with point systems for faults and set routines) might take some of the innovation and spontaneity out of it. The BBC reported that a

2014 online petition against the sport entering the Olympics received more than 3,300 signatures.

Furthermore, the mainstream acceptance of the sport displeases some skateboarders. They wear their underground appeal with pride and would hate to lose it. On the other hand, a shot at competing on a world stage entices some, including American pro skateboarder Chris Cole. "It would be absolutely incredible to compete at the Olympic Games," he told the BBC. "You have a bucket list in life of memories you'd like to make, and this is definitely one I'd like to have checked off my bucket list."

organization representing skateboarding in the United States should the sport be added to the Olympics.

GOING PRO

Being a pro skateboarder can be high pressure. You not only must land your best tricks in front of huge crowds, but you must also talk to the media, maintain a positive public image, and manage the big purses that some competitions can bring. The line between amateur and pro skateboarders is thin. By some definitions, "professional" means getting paid to compete. By others, pro skateboarders are only those who are qualified to enter "pro" contests, such as the huge Tampa Pro. However, some skaters that many would consider amateur do make money and compete in pro events.

Very good amateurs typically sign with a company that helps them to skate in bigger events and get sponsors. Then, the company usually decides when the skater is ready to turn pro. Mike Sinclair, the director of the skateboard distribution company Tum Yeto, was quoted by ESPN in an October 2011 article saying that the company owners and managers determine the right time: "It's all in the skater. If the skater is skating like a pro and handling himself like a pro, then it's time." Once skaters have turned pro, companies (especially board and skate gear companies) will pay them—both in money and in boards, shoes, shirts, hats, or anything else a pro skater could need. Professional skaters wearing or using the company's merchandise—such as wearing Vans sneakers or drinking a Red Bull—is the best advertising!

Some professional skaters start their dreams very early. Ryan Sheckler turned pro at age thirteen in 2003! However, because the sport is so dangerous and truly ever changing, many careers are cut short.

COMPETING INTERNATIONALLY

There are major competitions for both amateur and professional skateboarders all around the world. The X Games might be the best known to the general public, but it is only one of many competitions.

The Tampa Pro is one of the biggest skateboarding events of the year—and every year it's different! A new course is created at the Skatepark of Tampa for each annual event. The Mystic Sk8 Cup in Prague, Czech

Ryan Sheckler turned pro at thirteen years old, but his first gear contract happened when he was only seven! Skate companies are always looking for the next big pro skater.

EXTREME SKATERS

Some of the most exciting skaters in history are the ones competing today! These are some of the most popular contemporary skaters:

- Chris Cole landed his first corporate sponsorships at age sixteen. A daring street skater, Cole is known for trying tricks no one has done before and using any obstacle that can be skated or jumped on in unique ways. He won *Thrasher's* Skater of the Year award in 2005 and 2009, and he won the Super Crown Championship in 2013.

- David González is a professional skateboarder who grew up in Colombia and started skating at age ten. He became known for his part in *Thrasher's Possessed to Skate* video, which *Thrasher* described as González taking on the "gnarliest street spots in existence." He went on to win the magazine's Skater of the Year award in 2012.

- Ryan Sheckler started skateboarding as a toddler. His website states that he could land an ollie by age four! At his first X Games in 2003—the same year that he went pro at age thirteen—he was the only skater to land every trick that he attempted. In 2005, he became both National Street Champion and World Street Champion. Sheckler has racked up multiple firsts on the Dew Tour and has competed at the highest level internationally.

Republic, also has a new course built each year. The Mystic Sk8 Cup is one of the best European skateboarding competitions, and a victory there comes with a $40,000 prize!

WOMEN IN SKATEBOARDING

While men's skateboarding may be headed for the Olympics and seems to gain more legitimacy as time goes on, women's skateboarding continues to resemble more closely the underground skating of the 1980s. Far fewer women skateboard than men, and even fewer women successfully make a living on the pro circuit. In general, women skateboarders are still fighting for acceptance in a male-dominated sport. In a July 2014 article, Alana Smith, the first female skater to land a trick called the 540 McTwist in a competition, described the culture to *Forbes* magazine: "When people see girls skating, they don't see us as skaters. They don't think we take it seriously and are willing to go all out. But we are right underneath them working super hard to be where [male skateboarders] are at."

Some of this could be a result of the pressures that young women face in how they look and dress. *Huck* magazine reported that girls-only skateboarding company Hoopla was working to change the message that young girls were getting about what a skateboarder looks like. Hoopla cofounder Cara-Beth Burnside said that her company wants to "show girls doing what they love and still looking like girls… you don't have to wear a really short shirt or your bikini just to get attention."

Progress continues to be made. In 2010, Leticia Bufoni was the first woman to be signed to the Nike SB team, something that she told *Forbes* she never thought would happen. "It has put a crack in the door, and it is going to swing open after this," Hoopla cofounder Mimi Knoop, another professional skateboarder, said of Bufoni's addition to the Nike SB team. In addition, groups such as the Girls

Skating is not just a men's sport! Here, Leticia Bufoni wins gold in the Women's Skateboard Street Final competition at the 2013 X Games.

Skate Network and companies such as Hoopla, Girl is Not a 4 Letter Word (GN4LW), and Alliance are reaching out to young women interested in the sport.

As more and more people around the world try out a skateboard, more extreme tricks, daring stunts, and big personalities will emerge. Even though public interest has ebbed and flowed throughout the history of skateboarding, it now seems as though its place in action sports culture is here to stay. The only direction to move is up—whether that means higher vert ramps, more rotations, or wider gap jumps is up to the young skaters just starting to test their limits on a board.

GLOSSARY

axle A pin or shaft on which a wheel or pair of wheels turns.

ball bearing The part of a machine in which another part turns on metal balls that roll easily in a groove.

consciousness A collective awareness.

derive To come from a certain source.

emulate To be like or copy.

innovation The introduction of something new or the process of coming up with something new.

legitimate Generally accepted as having a rightful place.

notoriety The state of being widely known for a bad characteristic.

precursor Something that comes before another.

purse The money gained by winning a sporting event.

relevant Having significance on the matter or time at hand.

slalom Skateboarding in a zigzag pattern, often downhill, between obstacles or flags.

sponsor An organization that pays for and has a hand in planning an athlete's schedule.

turning radius The radius of the smallest circular turn that a skateboard or other vehicle is capable of making.

urethane A man-made compound used to make skateboard wheels.

vert Short for "vertical." An event in skateboarding involving a ramp and the skateboarder changing from horizontal movement to vertical movement to do a trick.

Board Rescue
200 Colorado Avenue
Palo Alto, CA 94301
(408) 515-7422
Website: http://www.boardrescue.org
Board Rescue donates skateboards and safety gear to groups that
    work with special-needs and underprivileged children.

Evolve Skate Camp
69 Wingold Avenue, Unit 120
Toronto, ON M6B 1P8
Canada
(416) 619-4521
Website: http://www.evolveskatecamp.com
Just like other sports, you can attend a camp to better your skate-
    boarding skills! Evolve is located in Toronto, Canada, and has
    both a summer camp and lessons available.

International Skateboarding Federation
P.O. Box 57
Woodward, PA 16882
(814) 883-5635
Website: http://www.internationalskateboardingfederation.com
The ISF strives to be the global governing body of competitive
    skateboarding and to bring the sport to a wider audience.

Skateistan
Oppelner Strasse 29
Berlin 10997
Germany

Website: http://www.skateistan.org

Skateistan is an international organization that uses skateboarding to help children get interested in education. It has a variety of leadership, cultural, and skateboarding experiences for youth.

Skate Like a Girl
158 Thomas Street
Seattle, WA 98109
(206) 973-8005
Website: http://www.skatelikeagirl.com

Skate Like a Girl works to bring skateboarding to girls and women of all backgrounds. It collaborates with groups in cities and communities to spread an inclusive and positive message about female skateboarding culture.

Tony Hawk Foundation
1611-A South Melrose Drive, #360
Vista, CA 92081
(760) 477-2479
Website: http://www.tonyhawkfoundation.org

The Tony Hawk Foundation focuses on bringing skateboarding opportunities to low-income areas, including building skate parks and supplying grants.

Vancouver Skate Coalition
2337 Main Street
Vancouver, BC V5T 3C9
Canada
(604) 708-5678
Website: http://www.vsbc.ca

The Vancouver Skate Coalition is just one organization working within a city to provide places to skateboard by rehabilitating old parks and unused areas as skate parks.

WEBSITES

Because of the changing nature of Internet links, Rosen Publishing has developed an online list of websites related to the subject of this book. This site is updated regularly. Please use this link to access the list:

http://www.rosenlinks.com/STTE/Skate

FOR FURTHER READING

Cobb, Allan B. *Skating the X-Games.* New York, NY: Rosen Publishing, 2009.

Hawk, Tony. *Between Boardslides and Burnout: My Notes from the Road.* New York, NY: ReganBooks, 2002.

Horsley, Andy. *Skateboarding.* New York, NY: PowerKids Press, 2012.

Louison, Cole. *The Impossible: Rodney Mullen, Ryan Sheckler, and the Fantastic History of Skateboarding.* Guilford, CT: Lyons Press, 2011.

Marcus, Ben. *The Skateboard: The Good, the Rad, and the Gnarly: An Illustrated History.* Minneapolis, MN: MVP Books, 2011.

Mortimer, Sean. *Stalefish: Skateboard Culture from the Rejects Who Made It.* San Francisco, CA: Chronicle Books, 2008.

Novak, Brandon. *Dreamseller.* New York, NY: Citadel Press, 2009.

Stecyk, Craig. *Dogtown: The Legend of the Z-Boys.* New York, NY: Burning Flags Press, 2000.

BIBLIOGRAPHY

Cave, Steve. "The True Story of Dogtown and the Zephyr Team."
    Retrieved September 10, 2014 (www.skateboard.about.com/od/
    boardscience/a/DogtownHistory.htm).

Curtis, Bryan. "Cheap Tricks." Outside, July 17, 2006. Retrieved
    September 21, 2014 (www.outsideonline.com/outdoor-adventure/
    Cheap-Tricks.html).

Glass, Alana. "Women's Skateboarding: Why It Matters to Skate Like a
    Girl." *Forbes*, July 15, 2014. Retrieved September 20, 2014 (www
    .forbes.com/sites/alanaglass/2014/07/15/womens-skateboarding
    -why-it-matters-to-skate-like-a-girl).

Guida, James. "Thirty Years of Skating." *New Yorker*, July 13, 2012.
    Retrieved September 5, 2014 (www.newyorker.com/culture/culture
    -desk/thirty-years-of-skating).

Kurland, Andrea. "Mark Gonzales Unrecorded Hearsay." *Huck*, Febru-
    ary 25, 2013. Retrieved September 4, 2014 (www.huckmagazine
    .com/ride/skate/mark-gonzales-2).

O'Neal, Devon. "Reflecting on Tony Hawk's 900." ESPN, July 17,
    2014. Retrieved September 1, 2014 (xgames.espn.go.com/events/
    2014/austin/article/10622648/twenty-years-20-firsts-tony-hawk
    -900).

Owen, Tony. "The Evolution of Skateboarding—A History from Side-
    walk Surfing to Superstardom." *Skateboarding* magazine, March 5,
    2013. Retrieve September 5, 2014 (www.skateboardingmagazine
    .com/the-evolution-of-skateboarding-a-history-from-sidewalk
    -surfing-to-superstardom).

Wisenthal, Lucas. "10 Innovations That Changed Skateboarding." Green
    Label, January 17, 2014. Retrieved September 6, 2014 (www
    .green-label.com/action/10-innovations-changed-skateboarding).

INDEX

A

Adams, Jay, 8
Alva, Tony, 8

B

Bachinsky, Dave, 28
Bennett Trucks, 15
Blind Skateboards, 24
Bones Brigade Video Show, 10
Brown, Jake, 20–22
Bufoni, Leticia, 38
Burnquist, Bob, 25–27

C

Cadillac Wheels, 7
Cole, Chris, 37
competitions, 36–38
culture, skate, 29, 30

D

decks, 13–15
Duffy, Pat, 20
Dyrdek, Rob, 31

E

El Toro High School stairs, 27–28
ESPN, 12

G

gear, 17–19
Gelfand, Alan "Ollie," 23
Girls Skate Network, 38–39

Gonzales, Mark "Gonz," 24–25
González, David, 37

H

half-pipes, 12
Hawk, Tony, 4, 5, 10, 12, 25, 27, 30, 34
helmet, 17, 20
history of skateboarding, 6–12
Homoki, Aaron "Jaws," 27
Hoopla, 38, 39

I

Independent Trucks, 15–17
injuries, 7, 19–22, 24, 27
International Skateboarding Federation, 31, 32, 33, 34

K

kicktail, 15, 23

L

laws against skateboarding, 29, 30
longboards, 17
Loop of Death, 25–27

M

Mullen, Rodney, 10, 30
Mystic Sk8Cup, 36–38

N

Nike SB, 31, 38
900 (trick), 4, 12, 25

O

ollie, 9, 15, 23, 28, 37
Olympics, 33–35, 38
organizations, skateboarding, 31–35

P

Peralta, Stacy, 8, 10
pro, going, 35–36

S

safety, 7, 9, 13, 20
    gear, 17–19
    tips for, 18
Schaar, Tom, 4
Search for Animal Chin, The, 10
Sheckler, Ryan, 36, 37
shoes, 17–19, 31
skateboards, evolution of, 6, 13–17
Smith, Alana, 38
Smithsonian Institute, 30
sponsorships, 35–36, 37
Street League Skateboarding, 31
street style, 10, 17, 23, 24–25
style/fashion, 29, 30
swimming pools, skateboarding in, 8, 9,
    10, 12, 24, 29

T

Tampa Pro, 35, 36
1080 (trick), 4

tricks, learning and building on, 23
trucks, 13, 15–17

U

urethane wheels, 7, 13
USA Skateboarding, 33–35

V

Vans, 19, 29, 36
vert skating, 9, 10, 12, 17, 23, 25
Video Days, 25
videos, skateboarding, 10, 25, 28

W

wheels, 7, 13, 15–17
Whitehead, Cindy, 30
women, and skateboarding, 30,
    38–39
World Cup Skateboarding, 31

X

X Games, 4, 20, 25, 29, 36, 37
    creation of, 12

Z

Z-Boys, 8, 9, 10, 12, 24

ABOUT THE AUTHOR

Kristen Rajczak is an editor at Gareth Stevens Publishing in Buffalo, New York, and a children's book writer. With a background in arts, writing, and reporting, Kristen finds the culture and style of action sports endlessly exciting and innovative. Her interest in the sport of skateboarding stems from watching the X Games as a child and teen. Since, she's been fascinated with the tenacity, fearlessness, and grit pro skateboarders use to seemingly defy gravity. In addition, Kristen's favorite video game of all time is *Tony Hawk: Pro Skater* for N64—she always played as Bob Burnquist.

PHOTO CREDITS

Cover, p. 4 (skateboarder) © iStockphoto.com/vernonwiley; cover, pp. 1, 3, 6, 13, 23, 31 (skateboard pipe) © iStockphoto.com/PPAMPicture; p. 5, 28 Rick Kern/WireImage/Getty Images; p. 6 (inset) Lambert/Archive Photos/Getty Images; p. 7 Manchester Daily Express/SSPL/Getty Images; p. 9 Ty Allison/Photographer's Choice/Getty Images; pp. 10–11 Rex Features/AP Images; pp. 14–15 underworld/Shutterstock.com; p. 16 Adrian Matthiassen/Shutterstock.com; p. 19 Doug Pensinger/Getty Images; pp. 20–21 © AP Images; p. 23 (inset)wavebreakmedia/Shutterstock.com; pp. 26–27 Buda Mendes/LatinContent WO/Getty Images; pp. 32–33 Nic Bothma/EPA/Newscom; p. 36 Lee Celano/WireImage/Getty Images; p. 39 © ZUMA Press, Inc/Alamy; cover and interior pages graphics SkillUp/Shutterstock.com, Sfio Cracho/Shutterstock.com, saicle/Shutterstock.com, Frank Rohde/Shutterstock.com, Thomas Bethge/Shutterstock.com, nortivision/Shutterstock.com, PinkPueblo/Shutterstock.com.

Designer: Michael Moy